# SUPER MARIO ODYSSEY

# Kingdom Adventures

*Travel Companion Volume 2*

**Lake Kingdom**
**Wooded Kingdom**
**Cloud Kingdom**

# Pack Your Bags!

When Mario set out to stop Bowser from forcing Princess Peach to marry him, he had no idea what it would lead to. But his attempt to save a friend quickly proves far more difficult than Mario could have ever anticipated. Much to Peach's dismay, the tuxedo-clad Bowser manages to knock Mario from his ship, sending him tumbling through the night sky.

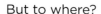

But to where?

Thanks to a friendly flying top hat known as Cappy, Mario is roused from his slumber in a tiny area of the Cap Kingdom known as Bonneton. The local population isn't just friendly, but they've got a stake in stopping Bowser too! One of their own, Cappy's sister Tiara, was also kidnapped, and he wants to team up with Mario to get her back.

With Cappy's help, Mario soon finds himself in command of the Odyssey, an incredible airship capable of traveling to more than a dozen kingdoms. From the scorching sands of Tostarena to the bustling streets of New Donk City, there's no place the Odyssey can't go. Don your favorite hat and put your seatback in its full, upright position. The Odyssey is taking flight for Mario's biggest, boldest adventure yet!

# CONTINUE THE ADVENTURE!

**Collect all six volumes of *Super Mario Odyssey: Kingdom Adventures* to follow Mario on his epic journey!**

Mario's desire to stop Bowser may be his ultimate goal, but the best part of any adventure is the journey, not the destination. And oh, the places you'll go, Mario!

Take us along as we help you uncover the secrets of three kingdoms in Mario's quest. The following pages contain insights into the most popular tourist attractions, regional events and activities, local culture, and souvenirs. Consider this book your ultimate travel companion, a tour guide designed to not only help you get the most out of your travels, but also a record of the memorable times you and Mario share.

This volume provides insights into the Lake Kingdom, Wooded Kingdom, and Cloud Kingdom. For gameplay assistance, maps of Power Coins, and general strategy, be sure to check out the *Official Super Mario Odyssey Strategy Guide*, sold separately.

# Lake Kingdom

## Land of Beauty and Clear Waters

Finding a dry place to land the Odyssey isn't easy, but the beauty of Lake Kingdom sure is worth the effort. The warm sand, colorful locals, and calm waters of the region immediately combine to put a traveler's mind at ease.

Connected by an underwater tunnel, the upper spillway serves as an intriguing introduction to the depths of Lake Lamode. There you find numerous native species, from a rainbow of tiny fish to the gentle blue giant, Dorrie. Cheep Cheeps also call the area home.

Of course, no conversation about Lake Lamode is complete without mentioning the stylish women of the water known as Lochladies. The Lochladies live in Water Plaza, a sprawling palace of intricately carved stone, kept dry by a magnificent glass dome. Lochladies can breathe both in and out of water, but they prefer to live on dry land—probably don't want to get their fashion magazines soggy.

Lake Kingdom is a tranquil locale, but it isn't without risk. Goombas and Mini Goombas are known to frequent the Courtyard area where, long ago, the Lochladies used to dye clothes. Elsewhere, in the underwater tunnel, an aggressive plant-like creature known as the Komboo may be encountered.

Travelers may not spend the bulk of their trip at Lake Lamode, but it's certainly a place worth visiting. It's the only place where tourists can swim with a giant Dorrie, unzip walls made of cloth, and dive into seemingly bottomless tunnels. But always remember, the Lochladies want to see you dressed to impress!

# Lake Lamode

## The town both in and on the lake dreams

| GET TO KNOW LAKE LAMODE | |
|---|---|
| Population | Middling |
| Size | Limited |
| Locals | Lochladies |
| Currency | Scale-Shaped |
| Industry | Clothing, Design |
| Temperature | Average 79°F |

The glamorous Lochladies are always happy to meet a visitor, especially if he's as well-dressed as Mario. The Lochladies can be found splashing, swimming, and strutting their stuff throughout the Lake Kingdom—and they're always up for a chat. As comfortable in the water as they are in Water Plaza, these fashionable women are sure to make a visit to the region memorable.

## THREE KEYS TO THE KINGDOM

 *Visit the Water Plaza, especially if you enjoy breathing air.*

 *Swim with the local Dorrie for an unforgettable experience.*

 *Admire the gown that qualifies as a national treasure.*

# Top Sights

## The Domed Water Plaza

Lake Lamode, the land of fashion. The underwater Water Plaza is protected by a glass dome, but don't worry, there's air inside to breathe.

When you look up at the lake from within the plaza, you can see Dorrie swimming amid the stunning scenery.

*Someone filled the elevator with water! #HoldYourBreath #SwimmingUp #WaterPlaza*

# WATER REPELLING BARRIERS

Nobody knows exactly how the doors work in the domed Water Plaza, but the large openings in the glass somehow keep the water out and the air in. You'll find openings on the first, second, and third floor. And also in a shaft that leads to the roof.

## Window Shopping

Considered the most luxurious garment this kingdom has to offer, the Lochlady Dress is displayed in the show window of the Water Plaza. Of all the garments created by the Lochladies, only the very best and most beautiful is selected for this great honor. It's a national treasure!

What's so special about a dress you can't even go snorkeling in? #DeepSeaCouture #LochladyDress #LakeLamode

It's said that wearing this dress brings eternal happiness, so naturally every bride yearns for it. Sadly, this lovely, one-of-a-kind item is not for sale.

## FASHION IS QUEEN

The Lochlady Dress isn't the only example of high fashion at Lake Lamode. The Style Sisters on the roof of Water Plaza are keen on rewarding anyone with a complete costume who happens to chat with them.

## Zippers of Mystery

Fitting of a kingdom famous for its fashion, you can find zipper art all over the place here. Zippers can be securely fastened as well as opened and closed freely, so perhaps they have a deeper meaning...

That said, this particular zipper is more than decoration. It actually works, so stop by and give it a try.

Some people dig up buried treasure, others unzip it. #SoggyZipper #LakeLamode #GoneSwimming

## ZIPPER BRIDGES

It should come as no surprise to learn that many of the walls in Lake Kingdom are made of fabric. Hence, all the zippers. The stylish cloth doesn't just hide secrets, but can even serve as a bridge when unzipped.

## Dorrie the Aquatic Buddy

This gentle creature spends its days swimming gracefully in Lake Lamode. If you're confident in your abilities, swimming alongside it might make for some wonderful memories. Keep an eye out for Dorrie-themed souvenirs, which tourists just love.

*Cheep Cheep and Dorrie at Lake Lamode. #BFF #FishGillsFTW #LakeLamode*

## DORRIE HAS COMPANY

Dorrie might not have as much room in Lake Lamode as the open ocean, but there are plenty of colorful fish to keep it company. Maybe Mario will run into other Dorries during his journey?

## Soaked in History

Once a spot for designers to relax and even dye cloth, this soaking pool has a rich history. Since most activity centers around the lake town, this is now a well-known fishing hole.

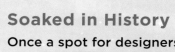

*Be careful with that hook, Lakitu! #NotAFish #SoakingHole #LakeLamode*

## SAFE FROM GOOMBAS

Usually a glowing spot on the ground means there's a Power Moon or coins nearby. Imagine Mario's surprise when three Mini Goombas popped out! Already injured, Mario was lucky to have the Soaking Hole close by—Goombas can't swim!

# It's-a-You, Here!

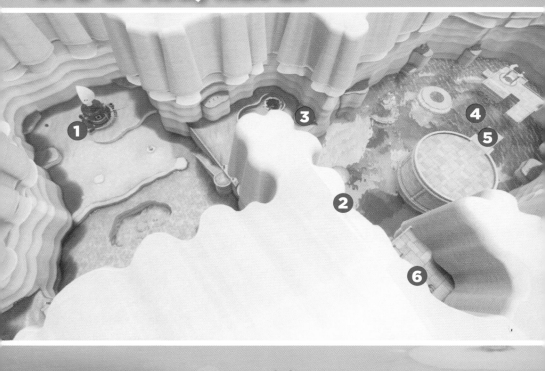

**The Odyssey:** The beach where the Odyssey lands is a very popular place for tourists and locals like!

**Underwater Entrance:** The entrance to Lake Lamode is a favorite place to swim for many of the area's Cheep Cheep population.

**Courtyard:** Expect to find a number of Goombas at the Courtyard. Whether they've come to watch Lakitu fish or because this is the highest, driest ground in Lake Kingdom, nobody knows.

**4**

**Water Plaza:** *Capable of keeping the water out and the air in, this feat of engineering serves as the main home for the Lochladies of Lake Lamode.*

**5**

**Water Plaza Terrace:** *What could such a large wide-open space possibly be used for? Whatever it is, you can bet Mario will find out.*

*6*

**Viewing Balcony:** *It's a mystery how to get to this special spot overlooking Lake Lamode, but the views can't be beat!*

## Souvenir Hunting

The Lochladies might be all about high fashion, but they want to see their guests dressed to go swimming. And that means a snorkel and float ring. Be sure to go diving for the 50 scale-shaped Regional Coins scattered throughout Lake Kingdom to purchase souvenirs at the Crazy Cap shop.

| CRAZY CAP: LAKE LAMODE EXCLUSIVES | |
|---|---|
| **ITEM** | **REGIONAL COINS** |
| Swim Goggles | 5 |
| Swimwear | 10 |
| Lake Kingdom Sticker | 5 |
| Rubber Dorrie | 5 |
| Underwater Dome | 25 |

## HAZARDS & HOSTILES

Lake Lamode has several hazards both in the water and out of it. While visitors are free from harm near the Odyssey and inside the Water Plaza, the outlying areas contain a host of minor dangers. The biggest, of course, is a simple function of Mario's biology: he doesn't have gills.

***Drowning:*** *By far, the biggest risk at Lake Kingdom is accidental drowning. No matter how well you think Mario can hold his breath, it's best to seek out air bubbles whenever they're available. Monitor his air level and come up to breathe whenever it turns red. Or, better yet, capture a Cheep Cheep and swim to your heart's content.*

***Komboo:*** *This aggressive cousin to kelp marches across narrow underwater corridors in an attempt to injure Mario through contact. Komboo aren't common at Lake Lamode, but they are a risk. Fortunately, Cappy is every bit as powerful underwater as he is on dry land. Toss him at the Komboo to cut them down.*

***Cheep Cheep:*** *The colorful Cheep Cheep aren't aggressive, but they can cause injury if Mario happens to swim into them. If you've got a long distance to swim (or a deep tunnel you want to dive to the bottom of), it's best to capture a Cheep Cheep.*

***Goombas:*** *Goombas prowl the Courtyard area, near Lakitu's fishing hole. Goombas can be captured, stepped on, or outrun, but you can't ignore them. They really don't like being ignored!*

***Mini Goombas:*** *Mini Goombas aren't out and about like their larger cousins, but they're there, hiding in the recesses and ready to jump out when Mario least expects it!*

## CAPTIVE FRIENDSHIPS

There are a number of things to capture at Lake Kingdom, including Goombas, Cheep Cheep, and the Binoculars on the beach near the Odyssey. But of all the things that Mario can capture, it's the Zipper that proves most useful.

***Zippers:*** *Zippers reveal hidden alcoves and secret entrances to mysterious areas that otherwise go unseen. All it takes to find them is a pull of a zipper.*

# Events and Attractions

## Koopa Freerunning

Mario won't have to go far from the Odyssey to participate in the Freerunning Race at Lake Kingdom. The race stretches from the beach by the Odyssey all the way to Water Plaza Terrace, but there won't be any stairs to help create an easy path. While the Koopas take to the underwater tunnel, champion freerunners know how to scale the wall without stairs.

## Art Appreciation

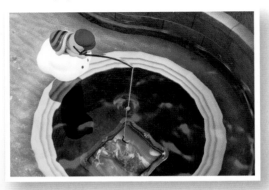

Be careful, Lakitu! Don't let those fishhooks scratch the painting! There's no telling how a painting of Sand Kingdom ended up in the bottom of the soaking pool at the Courtyard, but it explains how Lakitu ended up going fishing at the Oasis. Maybe a Cheep Cheep took up water colors?

## Postcards with Peach

The Lochladies aren't the only women Mario runs into at Lake Kingdom. Peach and Tiara eventually pay a visit to the area as well. Seek them out atop Water Plaza Terrace for a quick photo overlooking Lake Lamode.

# Local Advice

## No Stairs Necessary

It's possible to triple jump from the beach, toss the cap at the top of the wall on the left, dive jump, then tackle jump up to the landing. In fact, this maneuver is a key to winning the region's Koopa Freerunning event.

## Hold Your Breath, Mario

Mario can swim underwater for quite some time without coming up for air, but he does need to breathe. Fortunately, a circular meter appears next to Mario whenever he's underwater, indicating how much oxygen he has left. Best to swim through an air bubble, reach the surface, or capture a Cheep Cheep before the meter empties completely. Cheep Cheeps never have to worry about air.

# Wooded Kingdom

## Ancient Gardens Tended by Futuristic Machines

No adventure is complete without a visit to Wooded Kingdom, but it's not the towering trees that draw visitors from around the world. It's the flowers! Rising high above the forested hillside lie a number of impressive flower factories, fully-staffed by mechanized Steam Gardeners.

Steam Gardens has become a year-round travel destination for those wanting to sample the softer scents of nature. Its two sprawling flower fields are so revered, would-be brides flock to the facility to lay eyes on the Soiree Bouquet.

A visit to Steam Gardens isn't for the beginning traveler. The complex network of caves, paths, ramps, and lifts can prove challenging for those without a trusty guide. Set upon a mountainside, the location is also quite tall. It's certainly no place for those afraid of heights. Nevertheless, those who conquer their fears and pay a visit to the observation deck are rewarded with a view unlike any other.

Speaking of fear, there is an area of Wooded Kingdom that visitors are advised to avoid due to the overwhelming danger it presents. Nobody knows how it formed, or what purpose it serves, but far below Iron Road lies an area known as the Deep Woods. Not only are the Deep Woods home to a very aggressive T-Rex, but few have ever discovered a way to escape. Be very careful when walking along the edges, else you too may fall into the Deep Woods—and never be heard from again.

Visitors typically find the Wooded Kingdom to be a wonderful place to spend their time. Though the mechanical Steam Gardeners don't offer much in the way of entertainment—and the infrastructure is crumbling in spots—the natural beauty of the area keeps flower lovers coming back again and again.

# Steam Gardens

## The world's most advanced greenhouse

| GET TO KNOW STEAM GARDENS | |
| --- | --- |
| Population | Automated |
| Size | Deep, Wide |
| Locals | Steam Gardeners |
| Currency | Nut-shaped |
| Industry | Flowers |
| Temperature | Average 82°F |

## TENDING THE GARDEN

Wooded Kingdom is unique in that it has a local population, but one that is entirely robotic. Mario won't be able to converse with the Steam Gardeners, nor will they offer him any quests. They do, however operate the Crazy Cap store and make friendly comments as he passes by. So at least they're not rude.

## THREE KEYS TO THE KINGDOM

 *Smell the flowers. Not that you can miss them, but do savor the scent.*

 *Admire the Steam Gardeners and their impressive devotion to their work.*

 *Appreciate machines and nature living in exquisite harmony.*

Even the machines are shaped like flowers. #WoodedKingdom #TravelInspiration #Steam Gardens

# Top Sights

## The Living Factory

No one knows who built the giant machines dotting this land, but today the Steam Gardeners use them to maintain the greatest flower gardens in the world. The giant dome is climate-controlled and apparently self-sufficient, operating with no maintenance since ancient times.

## BALANCE BEAM COINS

It's certainly not for those who are afraid of heights, but Sky Garden is a great place to practice your balance! Best of all, there are some hidden coins sprinkled throughout the area. Regional Coins too!

## Guardians of Paradise

Visitors are welcomed not only by the humid air, but worker robots tending the flowers. They're known as Steam Gardeners, longtime residents of the kingdom.

You'll be impressed at how long they can work without rest, maintaining themselves perfectly. The robots love flowers—some grow them right out of their heads!

*Watch it, buddy! I'm walking here! #SpringShowers #GreenThumb, #SteamGardeners*

**A HELPING HAND**

Not that Mario couldn't find a way to the Mini Rocket on his own, but it sure was nice of the Steam Gardener to hold this ramp for him.

## Flowers as a Way of Life

While you see amazing flowers on any visit, you might be lucky enough to see the famous Steam Gardens Soirée Bouquet. It features giant white flowers that charm all who lay eyes on it. As you might guess from the name, it's by far the most popular bouquet for wedding ceremonies, sought after by wedding planners the world over.

*These flowers are almost as tall as Toad! #SkyGarden #WoodedKingdom #NoShorties*

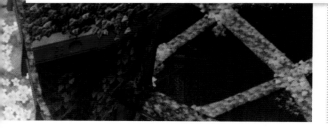

If Mario thought he'd be able to take a calming stroll in the Sky Garden, he's in for a surprise. The Sky Garden is never without a threat. The good news is that Mario can enlist the help of Goombas to eradicate the threat and restore the aromatic peace.

## A Deep Wood's Secret

It doesn't appear on any tours, but there is an area untouched by the machines of the Steam Gardens. Here the trees grow thickly, barely allowing any light through. The Steam Gardeners do not speak of it, but rumor has it that they discourage visiting this place because of the danger posed by the giant creatures that call it home.

*Nap time's over, this T-Rex doesn't look sleepy.*
*#TooScaredToMove #T-Rex #DeepWoods*

## IN TOO DEEP

A wrong step can land Mario in the Deep Woods, but it's going to take more than that to escape. Plant a seed in one of the pots to grow a beanstalk and climb it back to safety. Steam Gardeners stationed in the Deep Woods can help.

## A Growing Walkway

Be sure to try the system of paths called the Flower Road. You'll marvel at plants growing into temporary but walkable bridges. Watch your step, though—nature has no handrails.

*One minute you're just walking along, smelling the flowers. The next? No more flowers to walk on! #FlowerRoad #WoodedKingdom #AirWalking*

## FAST GROW CYCLES

The flower roads come and go quickly, but they'll always circle around. Once the P-Switch is hit flower road continues to travel f point to point, growing anew as as the destination is reached.

# It's-a-You, Here!

**The Odyssey:** *Mario sets the Odyssey down in a forested area of the aptly-named Wooded Kingdom, where a trail leads past dozens of towering trees toward the Steam Gardens plant.*

**2**

*Iron Road: Entrance:* Beyond a cave lies the base of an area known as the Iron Road, notable for its red maze of moving platforms and narrow ledges.

**3**

*Iron Road: Halfway Point:* Halfway to what? There's only one way to find out. Those who make it this far need only traverse the Flower Roads to see what lies in the distance.

**4**

*Sky Garden Tower:* The lower of the two domes is home to a beautiful field of flowers—and a commanding view of Wooded Kingdom. Daredevils can walk along the metal beams for an adrenaline rush!

**5**

*Forest Charging Station:* The middle floor of Steam Gardens is where the Steam Gardeners go to recharge their batteries. This area is also home to Goombas and Sherms so be careful!

47

**Summit Path:** *Those who venture this far up the mountain are in for a treat. Rocket Flowers grow in abundance along this trail, perfect for propelling Mario up the steep incline to the summit.*

**Iron Mountain Path, Station 8:** *This area is home to Uproots and another Sherm which can both be helpful for reaching the hidden alcoves tucked within the walls above, below, and under this part of the mountain.*

**Secret Flower Field Entrance:** *Access to the Secret Flower Field is heavily restricted. But the lucky few who gain admission are treated to one of the most beautiful floral displays in the world.*

**9**

**Observation Deck:** There's no easy way to reach the Observation Deck, but it's worth the effort. The truly daring can ascend higher into the clouds, or take flight with the Glydon who perches atop this incredible lookout.

**10**

**Iron Cage:** There's only one way in, and it's a bit further afield. Best to ask a city-dweller on how to reach this isolated location.

## Getting Around

Visitors to Wooded Kingdom do well to make use of the ample warp points that dot the region. Additionally, the previously discussed flower roads make it possible to reach areas that may at first seem inaccessible. But those aren't the only transportation options for Mario. Thanks to Cappy, Mario can also use the power of Rocket Flowers and slingshots (when available).

It's not uncommon for large rocks to fall from the mountain, blocking certain paths. Fortunately, the Steam Gardeners know to place slingshots in areas that could prove helpful when this happens. But don't worry, Mario always splashes down in the pond near Iron Road.

When you really want to get somewhere fast, give a Rocket Flower a try. These blooming boosts of power grow in the forest near the Odyssey and also along the Summit Path. Strap a couple on and see how fast Mario can run!

## Souvenir Hunting

The Steam Gardeners of Wooded Kingdom run a Crazy Cap store in the woods where the Odyssey lands and they don't just take standard coins, but nut-shaped Regional Coins too. The purple coins of Wooded Kingdom can be found in trees, caves, and everywhere in between. There are 100 Regional Coins to find—and spend—in Wooded Kingdom, so get looking! After all, one of the Steam Gardeners is very keen on those dressed in the Explorer suit. Be sure to wear it for a chance at a prized treasure.

| CRAZY CAP: STEAM GARDENS EXCLUSIVES | |
| --- | --- |
| **ITEM** | **REGIONAL COINS** |
| **Explorer Hat** | 5 |
| **Explorer Outfit** | 10 |
| **Scientist Visor** | 20 |
| **Scientist Outfit** | 25 |
| **Wooded Kingdom Sticker** | 10 |
| **Flowers from Steam Gardens** | 5 |
| **Steam Gardener Watering Can** | 25 |

## HAZARDS & HOSTILES

Wooded Kingdom is one of the most hostile regions Mario visits in his journey, thanks to the numerous creatures that call it home. Though many of them can be captured, Mario must be forever on guard at Steam Gardens, as the Steam Gardeners won't be able to help him if the local wildlife attacks.

*Uproot:* Uproots try and bash into Mario if they spot him, but they're mostly harmless. Toss Cappy at them to knock their helmet off, then throw him again to capture the Uproot. Capturing an Uproot is essential for reaching the many high ledges in Wooded Kingdom.

*Poison Piranha Plant:* Mario won't encounter too many Poison Piranha Plants—the Steam Gardeners do a very good job at pulling any noxious weeds they find—but they can prove troublesome. Though it is possible to capture them by throwing a rock into their mouth and then using Cappy to take control, it's best to just jump on their head.

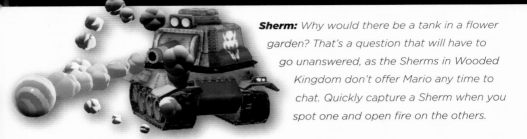

**Sherm:** Why would there be a tank in a flower garden? That's a question that will have to go unanswered, as the Sherms in Wooded Kingdom don't offer Mario any time to chat. Quickly capture a Sherm when you spot one and open fire on the others.

**Goomba:** Compared to some of the other threats lurking in Wooded Kingdom, Goombas are a welcome sight. Mario and Goombas have a long, shared history together, filled with bounces and ground pounds. Both of which work against Goombas, by the way.

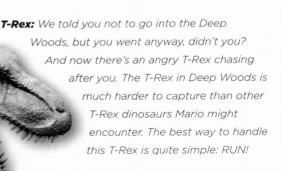

**T-Rex:** We told you not to go into the Deep Woods, but you went anyway, didn't you? And now there's an angry T-Rex chasing after you. The T-Rex in Deep Woods is much harder to capture than other T-Rex dinosaurs Mario might encounter. The best way to handle this T-Rex is quite simple: RUN!

**Fire Bro:** *The elusive Fire Bro resides in caves at Wooded Kingdom, sometimes behind locked doors. But make no mistake. This bouncing, fire-hurling cousin of the Koopa isn't just a menace. Fire Bros are spectacularly helpful when it comes time to light a campfire.*

## CAPTIVE FRIENDSHIPS

In addition to the many enemies that can be captured at Wooded Kingdom, there are a couple of creatures that don't pose any threat. These friendly beasts have unique abilities that stand to make Mario's time in Wooded Kingdom all the more memorable.

**Coin Coffer:** *Coin Coffers are notoriously tricky to spot, but Mario can find one in the Deep Woods and also near the entrance to the Secret Flower Field. Capture the semi-invisible creature to gain a wealth of coins— then spit them at everything in sight!*

**Glydon:** *High above the flower factories—and even above most trees—resides the Glydon. This spectacular flying lizard can be captured and taken for an incredible flight across the region. Visit Captain Toad, inspect hidden art, or just soar through the skies like a bird.*

# Events and Attractions

## Koopa Freerunning

Make your way to the Forest Charging Station to participate in a freerunning race along the Iron Road. The Koopas can get through the red maze pretty quickly, but there's an even faster way. Thanks to Cappy—and Mario's superb conditioning—Mario can traverse the course without capturing a single Uproot.

## Postcards with Peach

Peach made it to the top of the Observation Deck, a spot that offers one of the best views in the whole world. Toss Cappy at the scarecrow and scamper up the temporary platforms to reach her if you haven't been up that high before. But don't worry about finding a way down, the Glydon will help you with that.

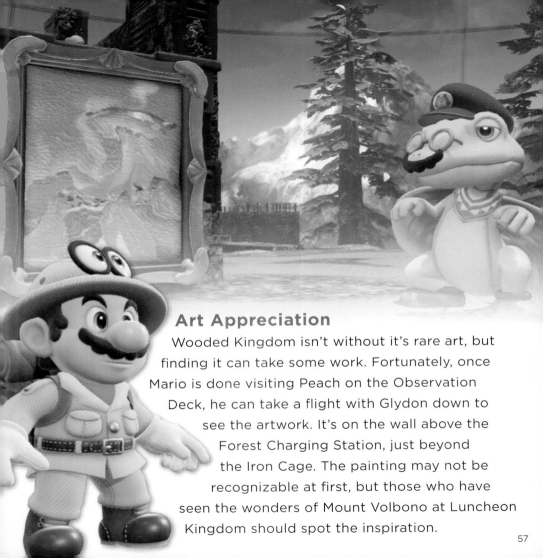

## Art Appreciation

Wooded Kingdom isn't without it's rare art, but finding it can take some work. Fortunately, once Mario is done visiting Peach on the Observation Deck, he can take a flight with Glydon down to see the artwork. It's on the wall above the Forest Charging Station, just beyond the Iron Cage. The painting may not be recognizable at first, but those who have seen the wonders of Mount Volbono at Luncheon Kingdom should spot the inspiration.

# Local Advice

## Beware the Deep Woods

Walk extra carefully along the edge of Iron Road, as one false step could plummet Mario into the Deep Woods, a mysterious, frightening place home to a very hostile T-Rex.

The Deep Woods contains plenty of treasure—there's no denying that—but many explorers have gotten lost exploring its depths. Your only escape is to plant a seed from a Steam Gardener in one of the many pots located there, and to climb the beanstalk back to safety.

## Rusty Metal Walkways

Be careful around the orange and yellow metal panels, as they are sure to collapse under Mario's weight. Lucky for Mario, those walkways somehow

## Use Those Warp Flags

Wooded Kingdom is undeniably the most complex of all the areas Mario visits in his journey. Myriad tunnels, ledges, and multi-tiered passageways make it difficult to know precisely how to get from one place to another. Visitors should seek out the warp flags to activate them for later use, saving much frustration down the road.

## The Return of Flower Road

The flower roads triggered by the P-Switches don't last forever, but they don't stay away either. Flower roads race by, lapping Sky Garden Tower continuously. If you miss one, just wait for it to pass by again. But double-check to make sure the P-Switch is pressed.

# Cloud Kingdom

## Mystery Above Our Heads

Some of the most memorable moments on a journey come when you least expect them, and sometimes from places you didn't even anticipate visiting. That can certainly be said for Mario's stop at Cloud Kingdom.

Cloud Kingdom isn't for the faint of heart, as life high above the clouds comes with an ever-present risk of falling, but it's a small price to pay to enjoy such serenity. And speaking of small, visitors should know ahead of time that Cloud Kingdom is the smallest of all the kingdoms visited by the Odyssey. But what it lacks in size, it more than makes up for with gorgeous scenery.

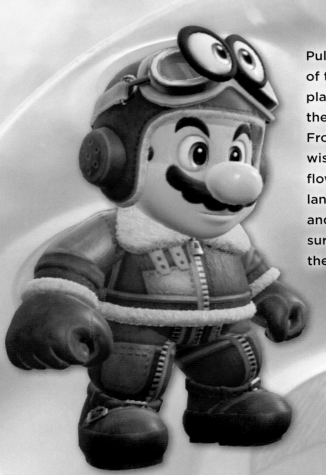

Pull up a seat atop one of the many moon phase platforms and revel in the splendor of the skies. From arching clouds to wisps of vapor that fall like flower petals, the pastel landscape of Nimbus Arena and its surroundings are sure to energize even the weariest of travelers.

Though some may find the quiet of Cloud Kingdom unsettling, visiting a location with no local currency or commercial business can be refreshing. It's a place left undisturbed, to be studied and appreciated by scientists and wanderers alike. Enjoy your time, take some photos, but please remember to leave only footprints.

# Nimbus Arena

## The archaeological dig site in the clouds

| GET TO KNOW NIMBUS ARENA | |
|---|---|
| Population | Unknown |
| Size | Unknown |
| Locals | Unknown |
| Currency | Unknown |
| Industry | Unknown |
| Temperature | Average 73°F |

Don't be disappointed if there's no friendly faces to greet you upon your arrival in Nimbus Arena. The Cloud Kingdom isn't home to a local population, nor has someone opened a Crazy Cap store in the vicinity. It's just a nice empty place to come and stretch your legs. Best of all, since you're above the clouds, it never rains!

## THREE KEYS TO THE KINGDOM

 *Navigate the vast sea of clouds that seems to go on forever.*

 *Feel the unyielding cloud-floor that won't budge no matter how you stomp.*

 *Explore the remnants of the civilization that once existed here.*

# Top Sights

## Life Above the Clouds

Perhaps everyone has had the experience of looking up at the clouds and imagining what it would be like to live among them. As it turns out, as fantastical as it may sound, there was once such a kingdom whose citizens looked down on the world from a fluffy, puffy paradise.

*Peach always said my head was in the clouds. Now it really is!*
*#NimbusArena #Daydreaming*

### A SEA UNFIT FOR SWIMMING

The blanket of clouds surrounding Nimbus Arena might look sturdy enough to walk on, but it's not. Mind the ledges around each of the islands, else this visit to Cloud Kingdom will be your last.

## Strange Floaty Material

While the particles that make up a cloud are extremely small and light, researchers have recently discovered a kind of cloud-like material that one can walk on. First discovered in Fossil Falls, this substance can change into and hold new shapes and even support weight.

The discovery prompted certain researchers to open an investigation into whether there might have once been a "cloud kingdom" in the sky.

The mysterious hats that spawn cloud platforms when struck don't last forever. After several seconds those platforms begin to blink. That's your cue it's time to jump before they retract into that wonderful hat shape.

*It really is a question what these ? hats are made of.*
*#Floating #CloudKingdom #DontLookDown*

69

## Vestiges of Greatness

Once researchers started looking for places in the sky, they quickly found a large platform of the levitating substance, dubbed Nimbus Arena.

Mysteriously, the land had markings that accurately showed the waxing and waning phases of the moon. Now, besides the obvious "how," researchers had to question "why?"

*The moon is out, time to sleep! #NapTime, #HalfMoon, #NimbusArena*

## TOP SECRET PLATFORMS

The platforms around Nimbus Arena aren't just for artfully illustrating the phases of the moon. They serve a purpose, too. But this isn't the place to discuss such sensitive matters...

## Giant Cloud Arches

Researchers are thus far baffled by the large cloud archway here. Some theorize that it's a kind of reticle that aligns with the moon. Some evidence suggests that the arch pulled this kingdom's Moon Rock to a specific location from the moon. The only certainty is that the Cloud Kingdom will continue to interest researchers for many years.

*Why didn't any coins come out? #PunchJump #NimbusArena*

## MOON CLOSE-UP

One of the joys of visiting Cloud Kingdom is seeing the moon up close.

The world sure is gorgeous up above the clouds.

## *Showers of Flowers*

The investigation is concluded now and yielded few undisputed facts. But the bits of cloud that fall like flower petals here make it the most dreamlike place you'll ever visit.

*Clouds fall like petals. Peaceful doves whiter than snowflakes. I feel out of place. #MarioHaiku, #ColorClash, #NimbusArena*

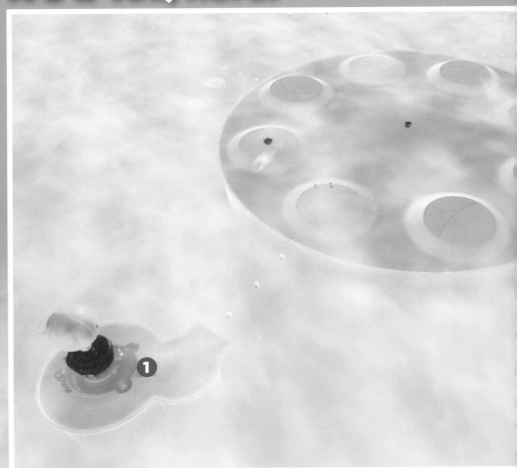

***The Odyssey:*** *Mario sets the Odyssey down just a few short hops from the main arena, where it will never be out of sight at tiny Cloud Kingdom.*

## Getting Around

Cloud Kingdom is the smallest of all the regions Mario visits, consisting of just a single circular arena with several small floating islands around its periphery. Visitors won't find any special transportation options here as everything is quite close. There are several platforms that fly into the air when struck with a ground pound. Aside from that, Nimbus Arena is your everyday, basic, kingdom in the skies.

## HAZARDS & HOSTILES

There is but one hazard in this tranquil landscape: falling. Watch your step around the perimeter of the arena and when leaping for the strange floaty cloud platforms. Be sure to hit them with Cappy before leaping, as it's a long way down if you mistime your leap.

# Events and Attractions

## Postcards with Peach

Funny seeing Peach up in the clouds, but here she is! And with Tiara too! The wonderful thing about Cloud Kingdom is that there's nothing

to distract visitors from their thoughts. It's the perfect place to relax and appreciate the beauty of the skies from a perspective seldom seen.

## Picture Match

Who said there weren't Goombas in Cloud Kingdom? Descend the warp pipe in the center of Nimbus Arena to test your memory—and fondness for Goombas—by completing a picture match puzzle! Study the picture then talk to Toad to start the game. Drag the puzzle parts onto the outline to recreate the Goombas as best you can.

# Kingdom Adventures

*Travel Companion Volume 2*

Written by Doug Walsh

DK/Prima Games, a division of Penguin Random House LLC
6081 East 82nd Street, Suite #400
Indianapolis, IN 46250

© 2017 Nintendo

ISBN: 9780744019315

Printing Code: The rightmost double-digit number is the year of the book's printing; the rightmost single-digit number is the number of the book's printing. For example, 17-1 shows that the first printing of the book occurred in 2017.

20 19 18 17    4 3 2 1

001-310363-Oct/2017

Printed in the USA.